I Bet Your Life

A Comedy in Two Acts

Fred Charmichael

A Samuel French Acting Edition

SAMUELFRENCH.COM
SAMUELFRENCH-LONDON.CO.UK

Copyright © 1995 by Fred Charmichael
All Rights Reserved

I Bet Your Life is fully protected under the copyright laws of the United States of America, the British Commonwealth, including Canada, and all other countries of the Copyright Union. All rights, including professional and amateur stage productions, recitation, lecturing, public reading, motion picture, radio broadcasting, television and the rights of translation into foreign languages are strictly reserved.

ISBN 978-0-573-69571-1

www.SamuelFrench.com
www.SamuelFrench-London.co.uk

For Production Enquiries

United States and Canada
Info@SamuelFrench.com
1-866-598-8449

United Kingdom and Europe
Theatre@SamuelFrench-London.co.uk
020-7255-4302

Each title is subject to availability from Samuel French, depending upon country of performance. Please be aware that *I Bet Your Life* may not be licensed by Samuel French in your territory. Professional and amateur producers should contact the nearest Samuel French office or licensing partner to verify availability.

CAUTION: Professional and amateur producers are hereby warned that *I BET YOUR LIFE* is subject to a licensing fee. Publication of this play(s) does not imply availability for performance. Both amateurs and professionals considering a production are strongly advised to apply to Samuel French before starting rehearsals, advertising, or booking a theatre. A licensing fee must be paid whether the title(s) is presented for charity or gain and whether or not admission is charged. Professional/Stock licensing fees are quoted upon application to Samuel French.

No one shall make any changes in this title(s) for the purpose of production. No part of this book may be reproduced, stored in a retrieval system, or transmitted in any form, by any means, now known or yet to be invented, including mechanical, electronic, photocopying, recording, videotaping, or otherwise, without the prior written permission of the publisher. No one shall upload this title(s), or part of this title(s), to any social media websites.

For all enquiries regarding motion picture, television, and other media rights, please contact Samuel French.

MUSIC USE NOTE

Licensees are solely responsible for obtaining formal written permission from copyright owners to use copyrighted music in the performance of this play and are strongly cautioned to do so. If no such permission is obtained by the licensee, then the licensee must use only original music that the licensee owns and controls. Licensees are solely responsible and liable for all music clearances and shall indemnify the copyright owners of the play(s) and their licensing agent, Samuel French, against any costs, expenses, losses and liabilities arising from the use of music by licensees. Please contact the appropriate music licensing authority in your territory for the rights to any incidental music.

IMPORTANT BILLING AND CREDIT REQUIREMENTS

If you have obtained performance rights to this title, please refer to your licensing agreement for important billing and credit requirements.

CHARACTERS

STACY KINGSLEY
GREGORY LARSON
MATTHEW STODDARD
LAURA PUDNEY
GERTA
BURTON FINLEY
HENRIETTA SQUIRES
IRA WATSON

TIME AND PLACE

The action of the play takes place in the living room of a New England house. The time is the present.

ACT I

Early evening in mid-summer.

ACT II

A short time later.

I BET YOUR LIFE

ACT I

SETTING: The living room of a modern house set in New England. U.C. there is a stairway leading L. to the upstairs, to the R. down a passageway and offstage is the front door. U.R. there is a closet with the door opening to the R. On the R. wall there is a pair of French doors opening on stage. This leads to a terrace, the main part of it being off stage D.R. . D.L. there is an archway to a dining room and presumably a kitchen beyond. There is a desk above this arch with a chair to the L. of it and a bench along its right side. C. there is a armchair with a small table to its L., a sofa is on S.R.. The room is obviously done in very good taste and reflects affluence but it does not have a lived-in look. The walls are pastel and the overall effect is light, airy, and comfortable. At the rise, the French doors are closed and the stage is dark except for some fading sun or early moonlight coming in through the doors.

At RISE: The front door is open which sends a shaft of LIGHT onto the upstage area. STACY KINGSLEY comes in U.C. She is an attractive secretary probably in her late twenties, vivacious with a good sense of humor. She carries a purse and an attaché case.

    STACY. *(Calls Back)* Come on in..
    GREG. *(Off stage outside.)* Is it dangerous?

STACY. Between the car and the front door I saw one moose and two mountain lions.//
GREG. (*Off stage.*) You kid?//
STACY. Yes, I kid. Make a dash for it.//
GREG. (*Off stage.*) It's too dark in there.//
STACY. I'm trying to find a light switch. (*she finds a bank of switches on the upstage wall and flips one which LIGHTS the room.*) There, come to the light of your life.//
GREG. (*Off stage.*) Is that you?//
STACY. Come and find out. (*Crosses into room.*) Say, this is really nice. You'll like it.//
GREG. (*Off stage.*) It's still dark there.//
STACY. (*She flips another switch and obvious outside LIGHTS illuminate out where the front door is and also the terrace area.*) How's that? Watch out for bears.//
GREG. (*Off stage.*) Bears sleep at night. (*STACY gives a small wicked laugh. .*) Don't they?//
STACY. (*Crosses to L. of desk.*) Get in here or I'll lock the door.//
GREG. (*Off stage.*) No, don't (*GREG LARSON comes in carrying two suitcase. He leans against the closet wall.*)//
(*GREG is in his thirties or so and is an astute businessman but also has a rather timid streak at times which almost overcomes his sense of humor. He puts the bags down..*) I should fire you.//
STACY. (*Purse and briefcase on desk .*) You can't. I run the office.//
GREG. I hate the country.//
STACY. Surprise. Surprise.//
GREG. Damn Matthew Stoddard.//
STACY. (*Goes D.L.*) Matt is your best friend.//
GREG. I need a new one.

STACY. .Just look around you. It is wonderful. It is beautiful. (*Flicks light switch by dining room and LIGHTS go on O.L..*) There's a dining room through here and probably a kitchen..

GREG. (*Comes down into the room.*) Can you send out for Chinese in the country?

STACY. (*Goes into dining room.*) That is a gorgeous breakfront and look at those Hitchcock chairs and that bay window. What a view.

GREG. (*D.L.*) It is night. You can't see the view.

STACY. (*Reenters.*) But I know it is beautiful. Mountains and valleys and all those trees.

GREG. A heaven for dogs.

STACY. (*To foot of stairs.*) What do you suppose is upstairs?

GREG. I bet it's gone.

STACY. What?

GREG. The upstairs. I've heard porcupines eat houses in New England.

STACY. (*Flips another switch and LIGHTS go on upstairs*) See, even electricity up here. (*Goes upstairs.*)

GREG. I'm glad Tommy Edison didn't stay in New Jersey.

STACY. (*Off stage.*) This is great. One - two- three -

GREG. (*At foot of stairs.*) What are you counting, raccoon corpses?

STACY. (*Off stage.*) Bedrooms. There are four of them.

GREG. And a bathroom? Tell me there is a bathroom. I will not go outside to -

STACY. (*Off stage.*) There are two bathrooms and the water runs.

GREG. Faucets or pumps?

STACY. (*Comes downstairs.*) Chromium faucets. I think Matt has made a real find.

GREG. Then where is he?

STACY. He'll be here. He said tonight is the wager of a lifetime.

GREG. He'd better show up. You don't have a chaperone.

STACY. I'm probably the only secretary off for a weekend whose boss is not going to make a pass at her.

GREG. You never know.

STACY. (*Goes and opens French windows.*) Yes, I do. You promised my mother.

GREG. She told you?

STACY. I'm only kidding.

GREG. So am I.

STACY. This is great. There's a neat terrace out here, chairs, tables -

GREG. (*Moves down.*) chipmunks, skunks -

STACY. Now, Greg.

GREG. Shouldn't you say Mr. Larson?

STACY. We're not at the office. I call you Greg at dinner, at the theatres, in taxis.

GREG. But we're in the country.

STACY. I'm sure it's most informal.

GREG. Like "How's the milkin', Clem?" or "Dipped any candles lately, Marthy?", that sort of thing?

STACY. You got it. (*Goes to the closet.*)

GREG. Why does Matt have to have this big mystery contest here? Why can't he make the bet in the city?

STACY.(*Looks in the closet.*) This is fun.

GREG. (*Sits on the bench.*) Yeah.

STACY. You know it is. You two love to make wagers. *(Goes to him.)* Didn't you bet him he wasn't good enough to appear at the Metropolitan Opera?

GREG. He cheated.

STACY. He won the bet. You should have seen your face when he walked on-stage carrying a spear.

GREG. But he didn't sing.

STACY. *(Goes above desk to the L..)* He appeared at the Met, that was the wager.

GREG. Semantics.

STACY. And what a prize, lunch anywhere he wanted.

GREG. Only Matt would pick that stupid little waterfront restaurant.

STACY. But in Bermuda.

GREG. A bet is a bet and the conch soup was to die for.

STACY. *(Glances at phone pad and looks in desk drawers.)* You see.

GREG. But what is the bet and why are we trapped amongst Mother Nature's goodies?

STACY. *(Pulls out phone book.)* He said we'd find out and I imagine we shall.

GREG. He's just mad because I wouldn't push his script to the studios.

STACY. I think it's very good.

GREG. That's because you like him. He is the best soap opera writer in the business but as to screenplays, no way. The entire premise is not possible.

STACY. I think it is.

GREG. You're not the agent.

STACY. And you're not the writer, Matt is.

GREG. But I know what will sell.

STACY. His script should be in Hollywood right now.

GREG. And my reputation would be down the drain and you would be standing on the unemployment line.

STACY. (*Picks up attaché case from desk and goes U.C.*) You're impossible. Let's get the bags upstairs. I hate clutter. (*Picks one up.*)

GREG. Don't leave me here alone.

STACY. (*Goes upstairs.*) Scared?

GREG. (*Picks up bag and follows her.*) It's the air. I can't breathe. I'm used to second hand smog.

(*MATTHEW STODDARD appears at the windows. He is a contemporary of the others and perhaps more devil may care than GREG. He crosses to the stairs, looks up them, and howls like a wolf.*)

GREG. (*Off stage.*) What was that? (*MATT goes into the closet.*)

STACY. (*Off stage.*) The Hound of the Baskervilles.

GREG. (*Comes downstairs.*) Shouldn't we call a Forest Ranger or a Mountie?

STACY. (*Comes downstairs.*) Canada is still one hundred and fifty miles that way. (*Points.*)

GREG. (*As MATT gives another howl from the closet.*) Good God, it's the ghost of Benedict Arnold.

STACY. (*Hides behind him.*) I'm scared.

GREG. You are not and I am not (*Loudly at the closet door.*) and you can come out now, Matthew Stoddard. (*Opens the door and crosses R. MATT is standing there.*)

MATT. No surprise, huh?

GREG. None. (*MATT closes door.*)

STACY. (*Goes down by the bench.*) And I acted so scared.

GREG. You deserve an Oscar.

STACY. Come on, Greg, you were a little nervous.

GREG. (*Goes to the windows.*) I am always nervous in the country, all those trees but the only green I admire is in my wallet. This is your idea, Matt. I came. I saw. I have conquered. Is this the end of the wager?

MATT. (*Goes below sofa.*) No, it's about my script.

GREG. You are my best friend and I -

MATT. And you are my best friend and I can still go to another agent.

GREG. You are under exclusive contract to me.

MATT. I'll break the contract.

GREG. I'll call F. Lee Bailey.

MATT. You wouldn't?

GREG. Tell him, Stacy.

STACY. He would.

MATT. I know you would.

GREG. Then let us not argue. (*Goes below him to C..*) Let us go back to the city and spend a nice weekend at the Club which overlooks steel skyscrapers.

MATT. No, I conned you into coming up here for the biggest wager of our lives.

GREG. So what's the bet?

MATT. Let's get back to my screenplay.

GREG. Must we?

MATT. It hinges on that.

STACY. If I may interrupt -

GREG. Just once.

MATT. Only once.

STACY. (*Goes to MATT.*) I like your screenplay very much, Matt. It is exciting, suspenseful, and has a great twist ending.

MATT. Thank you, darling. Will you marry me?

STACY. Only if I don't have to sign a prenuptial agreement.

MATT. The offer is hereby withdrawn.

GREG. (*Goes to bench.*) If you two will stop trying to be witty and, oh, so Noel Coward, I would like to hear the rules of the bet.

MATT. (*Goes C. and STACY perches on the sofa arm.*) This house belongs to a friend of a friend of mine who, as we speak, is doing Europe.

GREG. I wish I were doing Time Square.

MATT. He rents this place out for weekends to friends and this is the perfect place for our wager.

STACY. (*Nods.*) Perfect.

GREG. Do you always have to agree with him?

STACY. I do when he is right.

MATT. Which is most of the time. To get back to my script -

GREG. I need a drink. There must be a bar. No friend of a friend of yours would have a house without a bar.

STACY. (*Rises and crosses in.*) There is one in the dining room. It is exquisite. It has a marbled top and is paneled -

GREG. Just get me a drink. You know what.

STACY. (*Goes D.L..*) Yes, sir. I obey. (*Turns in arch.*) But, starting now, I am on overtime. (*Exits.*)

MATT. She's so cute.

GREG. So is Miss Piggy but go on with the bet.

MATT. You think the premise of my script is all wrong, right?

GREG. Right. It is wrong. (*Sits on the bench.*) It's just implausible. A terminally ill man is too much of a chicken to kill himself so he hires a hit man to do it and then he finds he was misdiagnosed but who is the hit man? Right?

MATT. (*Goes to the windows.*) More or less.

GREG. (*Crosses U.C..*) Matthew, you are very successful. You make a fortune. You are envied by every housewife who answers those "be an author" ads in the magazines. Why can't you stay where you are?

MATT. To stay where you are is to move backwards. Someone said that, Confucius or someone.

GREG. (*Goes L. of chair C..*) Probably Sidney Sheldon. Your script is just not a plausible idea.

STACY. (*Returns with a highball.*) This conversation has not progressed.

GREG. (*Takes the drink.*) I need that.

STACY. Matt?

MATT. Not till I start the bet.

GREG. (*Sits on the bench.*) Shoot.

MATT. That is precisely it. Shoot. That is the bet.

STACY. (*Sits on the desk chair.*) This is getting good.

GREG. What is the bet?

MATT. (*Crosses C..*) I bet you that my script is exceedingly plausible. I have hired a hit man to kill you and the bet is that you can't spot him before you are dead.

STACY. You are joking, aren't, you?

MATT. Nope.

GREG. (*Not believing him.*) And how did you find a hit man, advertise in the Wall Street Journal or look in the Yellow Pages under "H"?

MATT. I did what they do in those movies like the one I have written and which you do not believe in.

STACY. Touchè.

MATT. I put on my worst clothes and I went from one seedy bar to another.

GREG. Your usual typical evening.

MATT. Keep joking. You'll stop soon enough.

STACY. I think he's serious.

GREG. You're not?

MATT. I am.

GREG. He is.

STACY. This is like your script.

MATT. I kept staying I wanted to get in touch with someone who could do something for me. I put "something" in quotes and said it quietly and ominously.

GREG. And the first person you met said he would snuff me out for a few dollars, right?

MATT. Wrong.

STACY. Don't interrupt, Greg.

MATT. (*Crosses below sofa.*) I did my ominous bit in several bars and left my phone number and guess what?

GREG. Jimmy Hoffa called from the beyond?

MATT. (*Goes L. and to above sofa.*) I got only one call.

GREG. Did you tape it? That's the proof you're not kidding.

MATT. The proof is coming tonight.

STACY. Here?

MATT. I met this gentleman who called.

GREG. This alleged man you hired to kill me is a gentleman?

MATT. (*Crosses down.*) I must say my script cast the big boss all wrong.

GREG. You admit you were wrong?

MATT. He fit in perfectly in the Oak Room at the Plaza. He looked like any corporate executive. I felt if I were buying controlling interest in General Motors.

STACY. Just my type. Is he married?

MATT. I didn't ask. I don't even know his name other than Mr. B.

GREG. Mr. B.? Well, you spin a good yarn.

MATT. I'm still spinning. He asked me what sort of killing I wanted.

STACY. You have a choice?

MATT. (*Goes above desk.*) It's like being in a Chinese restaurant. I could choose from columns 1, 2, or 3 and so on.

STACY. Killings with or without MSG?

MATT. I told him my whole scheme and he was most intrigued.

GREG. So am I.

MATT. (*Crosses by bench.*) I said I had a friend -

GREG. Me?

MATT. You, and this friend is terminally ill but didn't have the courage to end it all so my friend asked me to arrange it for him.

GREG. As a birthday present?

MATT. I'm so fond of you that I picked the most expensive killing. It's very civilized. It's called "Death at a Party".

STACY. (*Rises.*) We're having a party tonight? Goody.

MATT. (*Goes above sofa..*) All I had to do was provide the setting. Mr. B. said he would provide the guests.

GREG. Straight from which detention center?

MATT. Some local guests and some not.

STACY. How democratic.

MATT. (*Goes R. of sofa.*) And when the party is at its height and my friend is happy the end will come. Bang.

STACY. (*Goes above desk.*) Matt, you'll lose not only a friend but a top agent.

MATT. Can't be helped but there is an out clause.

GREG. There had better be.

MATT. (*Crosses in.*) Naturally, Mr. B. is not the hit man. He's like a producer. He hires the cast.

GREG. And fires them?

MATT. If the bet is over by ten o'clock which, of course, it will be.

GREG. (*Rises, puts glass on small table, and goes to MATT.*) Let me get this straight. If I spot the hit man then I win and if I give up I tell you before ten o'clock -

MATT. And I call Mr. B. and stop the game.

STACY. And if you don't call him?

MATT. Then it's bang-bang.

GREG. (*Goes to windows.*) All this to prove your script is plausible? You must be desperate.

MATT. You have no idea. I have been writing that soap opera for years. This script should be a stepping stone to being a really recognized writer. I know it is good.

GREG. This is some wager.

MATT. Mr. B. said he will be - how did he put it? - in the vicinity in his limo with the cellular phone.

GREG. I suppose the license plate says H-I-T?

MATT. Actually it is very conceited, just two initials, M. and E.

GREG. Why can't he be the hit man?

MATT. He's an executive. He doesn't do the work himself. And if I know who he is -

STACY. (*Sits on bench.*) Or she. Remember in those mysteries it's always he or she.

MATT. If I know I'm sure I would give it away.

STACY. Well, when does the party begin? I wonder what a hit man looks like?

(*LAURA PUDNEY appears at windows. She is of indeterminate age and very local and folksy, a real native. She carries two paper shopping bags loaded with food..*)

LAURA. Here I am.

STACY. Good grief!

GREG. What do you want?

LAURA. To do my job.

GREG. You're it! (*To MATT.*) I won the bet. Let's go back to the city.

LAURA. You ain't leavin' till you eat. I'm here to cook supper.

STACY. Oh, of course, the party dinner.

LAURA, (*Indicating bags.*) Nope, supper. That's what these are full of.

STACY. Here, let me help you. (*Takes one of the bags from her.*)

LAURA. That's right friendly of you.

STACY. The men are too tired to move.

LAURA. It's too hot for a roast and it's too late for a stew so I figured a nice cold supper.

STACY. Is that what was ordered?

LAURA. Employer said it was up to me.

GREG. (*Steps in.*) Who is the employer?

LAURA. Don't know. Stopped by the General Store and left some money for someone to cook supper tonight.

MATT. Nice try, Greg.

STACY. How many are expected?

LAURA. Oh, somewhere between six and eight. I have to be out of here by ten o'clock. I better get a move on. Where is the kitchen?

STACY. (*Crosses to arch D.L.*) Follow me.

GREG. You haven't worked here before?

LAURA. Not this place, no.

STACY. It's new to us but if you need any help just call and we'll figure it out between us.

LAURA. That's real nice of you. Oh, my name's Laura Pudney.

STACY. Laura? What a pretty name.

LAURA. It's from that song. My mother said I looked like a face what was passin' through on a train. (*Exits followed by STACY who gives a backwards glance.*)

GREG. (*Following them a few steps.*) She could be a hit man.

MATT. (*Sits on the sofa.*) She could be Amerlia Earhart.

GREG. Since she doesn't know the house, do you suppose she's one of Mr. B.'s people?

MATT. Possibly. Do you choose her? If you do and she is real and not the hit man then I win the bet.

GREG. Give me a little more time.

STACY. (*Reenters.*) I love her. She is right out of Central Casting.

GREG. (*Moves D.C..*) You really think so?

STACY. Either that or she was born and raised right here.

LAURA. *(In archway.)* You city folks allergic to anything?

GREG. Just guns.

STACY. He's joking. No, Laura, we eat anything.

LAURA. That's good because there ain't no choices. *(Starts to go but turns back.)* I should apologize for not bein' here sooner but there's a whole passle of police down the road..

GREG. What for, a shooting?

LAURA. Car wreck. Rescue squad and all is there. Took some folks off to the hospital. Shouldn't drive them big limousines on these roads. Too many curves.

MATT. *(Rises.)* A limousine?

LAURA. Yep, one of them long ones. Odd license plate, just two initials. M and E. *(Exits.)*

GREG. *(Goes U.C. to leave.)* That does it. The hit man's in the hospital. The bet if off.

MATT. No way. Mr. B. may be in the hospital but the hit man is on his way.

STACY. Or is here already.

GREG AND MATT. In the kitchen?

STACY. *(Sits on the bench.)* No, I would trust Laura Pudney.

MATT. That's what all those bank tellers said about Bonnie and Clyde.

GREG. *(Goes down to MATT.)* Isn't it time to return to the dangers of the city.?

MATT. Not possible. Mr. B. said he would make certain no one leaves till ten o'clock.

GREG. What does "make certain" mean?

MATT. It means someone is planted on this hill to make sure of the contract.

STACY. An understudy hit man?

GREG. (*Crosses down.*) Who might get his day.

MATT. I'm going down the hill and see what happened. (*Goes U.C.*)

STACY. But the understudy will kill you.

MATT. I'm safe. They have Polaroid's of me.

GREG. Lucky you.

MATT. Boy, I'm sure glad I'm not you. (*Exits.*)

GREG. He's my best friend.

STACY. (*Crosses C..*) He seems very worried.

GREG. (*Sits right of sofa.*) Then we're trapped.

STACY. No, you're trapped.

GREG. (*After a pause.*) I wish you'd say something.

STACY. Like what?

GREG. Like "let's get out of here." There must be some way.

STACY. (*Sits beside him.*) You wouldn't welch on a bet would you?

GREG. No - yes. Anyway, Matt is only kidding, isn't he? (*Pause.*) I'm sure he is. (*Pause.*) Aren't you sure? (*Pause.*) No, he is not kidding.

STACY. I knew you could answer yourself.

GREG. Maybe I should dress up in Laura Pudney's clothes and they'd never suspect. It always works in the movies.

STACY. You would leave that cook standing there in the kitchen naked?

GREG. She could wear a dish towel or a potholder or something.

STACY. And you'd leave me here alone with a killer on the prowl?

GREG. (*Rises and tries to pull her up.*) No you're coming with me.

STACY. And leave poor Matt holding the bag? No, sir.

GREG. (*Moves away R..*) You like him more than you do me. You always have

STACY. That is not the point.

GREG. It is the point. It has been the point for months. We both make plays for you and we both get nowhere.

STACY. What do you do, compare notes in the locker room?

GREG. If we did, we'd both lie so we never discuss you.

STACY. (*Leans back on the sofa with fake seduction.*) Why is it my curse to be this desirable creature?

GREG. (*Goes above sofa.*) You are right. Why didn't I hire someone from the senior center, someone with gray power?

STACY. And I could be secretary to some tottering old executive, marry him, poison him, and inherit his estate.

GREG. (*Goes C.*) You read too many scripts.

STACY. (*Rises.*) You know that I like you and Matt equally. You are both very nice but you are both a lot of talk.

GREG. (*Advances on her.*) Talk, am I? I'll show you talk, I'll show you -

GREG AND STACY. - my verbs and dangling participles, Mona.

STACY. (*Laughs.*) Mona?

GREG. I mean Stacy.

STACY. Caught you.

GREG. That was from Matt's soap last week, wasn't it?

STACY. I fought with him over that line and it still doesn't play well.

GREG. I was rather seductive though, wasn't I?

STACY. (*Pats his cheek.*) No, dear Greg, you were not. (*Moves away below sofa.*) I think we three should remain the best of friends as we are now.

GREG. (*Moves into her.*) Friends?

STACY. But I want you both to keep trying to be more. That's what makes this such a wonderful job.

MATT. (*Comes rushing in U.C.*) It's true. The wreck.

GREG. Did you see Mr. B.?

MATT. He was taken to the hospital.

STACY. Serious?

MATT. They said he was in shock, a temporary coma.

GREG. (*Crosses U.C..*) Then the bet is off. I'm leaving.

MATT. You can't. As long as he is in a coma we don't know who he hired for this job. Whoever the hit man -

STACY. - or woman -

MATT. Whatever. The hit person will act at ten o'clock.

GREG. It could be anyone.

MATT. (*Crosses below desk.*) It must be Laura.

STACY. (*Goes above sofa.*) Doubtful.

GREG. (*Crosses to MATT.*) She's the only stranger.

MATT. So far.

STACY. That's right, others are coming.

GREG. And one of them wants me dead.

(GERTA appears in the French windows. She is a very intense young woman wearing a long skirt, a loose shirt, sandals and has long hair. She is carrying a huge manuscript of a very long book which is well worn. She speaks and moves with great intensity.)

GERTA. (*Sweeps in below sofa.*) Which of you is Gregory Larson?

GREG. (*Crosses in pointing to MATT.*) He is.

MATT. I am not.

GERTA. (*Goes to him going below GREG and stares.*) No, you write that trash.

MATT. Yes, that's me, the trash writer.

GERTA. (*Turns to GREG.*) Then you are Mr. Larson?

GREG. There's no other man present.

GERTA. Then I have something for you.

STACY. (*Goes C.*) I don't like this.

GERTA. It's loaded.

MATT. Look out!

GREG. (*At the same time as he ducks behind chair C.*) Take cover!

GERTA. (*At the same time as she holds out the script.*) Here it is!

MATT. (*Grabs the book from her.*) Give me that!

GREG. It's a bomb!

GERTA. It certainly is not.

STACY. (*She has been calm and come below sofa.*) Hold it! Everyone desist! Shut up! (*They all stop and stare at her, GREG stands.*)

GERTA. (*Points at STACY.*) I know you.

STACY. And I know you.

MATT. Sorority sisters per chance?

GREG. (*Moves R. of chair C.*) I know when you open that the pages are cut out and there is a gun in there.

STACY. (*Crosses to MATT.*) Nonsense. (*Takes script from him.*) Give it to me.

MATT. Be careful.

GREG. Stacy, watch out.

STACY. (*Opens script.*) There. It is only the manuscript of a book. (*Hands it back to MATT.*)

GERTA. It is more than a manuscript. It is the survival of mankind as we know it.

GREG. You're an author?

GERTA. The Pulitzer, The Nobel will not change me.

MATT. Stay just as you are.

GERTA. You would know me if she would have let me see you.

STACY. This young woman, Gerta Something-or-other -

GERTA. Just Gerta. Last names are irrelevant.

STACY. Gerta Irrelevant has been coming by the office for the last week.

GERTA. I am pleased you are on the 31st floor. I belong to no fitness club. I walk those stairs for exercise.

GREG. Up and down?

MATT. Round trip?

GERTA. To bring you this I would climb Mount Everest barefoot.

MATT. What exactly is it other than a doorstop?

GERTA. It is a textbook for the future, outlining the mistakes of everyone from Jean Paul Sartre to Albert Einstein.

MATT. (*Hefting the script.*) They must have been powerful wrong.

GREG. (*Goes below GERTA to STACY.*) I am sure that Miss Kingsley here will see that we read it. Stacy, why have you not taken it before?

STACY. (*Takes script from MATT.*) I am very polite to young authors, aren't I, Ms. Gerta?

GERTA. Polite, yes. Helpful, no.

GREG. Of course I shall read it, shan't I, Stacy?

STACY. (*Hands script to him and goes to desk.*) Open it. Go ahead.

GREG. (*Opens the book.*) All right.

GERTA. You have just opened the answer to the question.

MATT. But he didn't ask a question.

GERTA. I mean the question, the one we all ask.

MATT. Oh, that question.

GREG. (*Tries to focus on the writing .*) What is this? Sanskrit?

GERTA. (*Goes to him.*) I write with a quill.

MATT. Plucked from your own head?

GERTA. (*Turns on him and crossed to him intensely.*) And you use a computer and pollute the environment when you write those daytime travesties. Your opinion is trash. Your scripts are trash.

MATT. You are quoting from the New York Times.

GREG. (*Hefting the book.*) You honestly wrote all this with a quill and a bottle of ink?

GERTA. It was good enough for Ludwig von Beethoven.

GREG. He wrote music.

MATT. He was deaf.

GERTA. My writing is music to the ears of those who understand.

STACY. (*Comes down between GERTA and GREG.*) There are ads for typists in all those "how-to-write-and-be-published" magazines so you call one of them and when it is typed neatly I am sure Mr. Larson will read it. (*Takes the script.*)

GERTA. No. (*Grabs it back. To GREG.*) We will experience it together. I will sit at your feet and read it aloud.

GREG. I'm rather busy this evening. I'm going to be shot.

GERTA. That is humor, I assume.

GREG. That is truth.

GERTA. (*Goes to the windows.*) I will wait outside. I will wait forever until you are ready. You have but to say, "The moment is now" and I shall appear. (*Exits.*)

MATT. Like Banquo's ghost?

GREG. (*STACY goes to the windows.*) Maybe she's a reincarnation of Houdini.

STACY. She is curling up under that tree. I think she is moaning.

MATT. I have been known to moan when I read my own writing. (*Sits on the bench.*)

STACY. If she's the hit person then this must be her first job.

GREG. (*Suddenly serious.*) Matthew.

MATT. (*Takes up his tone with a smile.*) Yes, Gregory.

STACY. Using full names, you are serious.

GREG. Time to stop this ridiculous charade. I can prove this whole evening is a joke.

MATT. You can?

GREG. Yes, I can.

MATT. How?

GREG. To hire a hit man must cost money and you didn't pay him, did you? (*Sits in chair C.*)

MATT. You're right, I didn't.

GREG. So there.

MATT. (*Rises.*) But you did.

GREG. I never -

STACY. Oh-oh.

GREG. Stacy, that "oh-oh" sounds very ominous.

STACY. (*Goes below sofa. To MATT.*) So that's why you wanted that check.

GREG. What check?

STACY. (*To GREG.*) I wouldn't have done that for anyone else, of course, but -

GREG. Done what?

STACY. He said it was for a joke and I know you play tricks on each other and - well - (*She runs out of steam.*) he is your best friend and - well -

GREG. The one you trust the least.

STACY. (*Moves away below sofa.*) Matt, help me before I'm fired.

MATT. I had to prove to this gentleman I was serious. I had to give him something more than a down payment.

GREG. You made a down payment on my death?

MATT. Just one thousand dollars.

GREG. With my own check?

MATT. No, with my own cash.

GREG. Then what check are you talking about?

MATT. He had to see me send off a legitimate check to a Swiss bank and I said I would give him the number of the account tonight at one minute after ten.

GREG. He swallowed that?

MATT. He said if the account number was wrong then I would wear cement Gucci's.

GREG. (*Rises and goes to STACY.*) How much was this check for?

STACY. You know how I give you all those checks to sign and you never really look at them closely and -

GREG. How much was it for?

STACY. - it was only for this bet and -

GREG. How much?

STACY. (*In a small voice.*) Fifty thousand. (*Sits.*)

GREG. Dollars?

MATT. It won't ever be cashed.

STACY. I put a stop payment on it right after I wrote it.

GREG. (*Turns to MATT.*) What about the cement Gucci's?

MATT. If we call it off before ten o'clock then I only have to make another small payment. Nothing to worry about.

GREG. (*Sits by STACY.*) As long as Mr. B. comes out of his coma quickly and calls off this person.

MATT. I've heard of some shock patients who couldn't communicate for months.

STACY. Isn't it exciting?

GREG. I do not believe someone is coming here tonight with the intention of killing me.

MATT. All you have to do is find him. This is a better prize than even that Bermuda trip. I bet your life.

STACY. And if you drop out of the game you lose.

MATT. But remember, when you decide my script is plausible we call off the hit person.

GREG. Unless I identify him first.

MATT. Right. (*Crosses above him to sofa.*) I hope you're having a good time. This took weeks to arrange. Mr. B., needed time to round up the guests.

STACY. And among them you have to find guess who?

LAURA. (*Enters from dining room carrying a colorful tablecloth and goes to windows.*) Pardon me. I'm just passin' through.

STACY. Like the face on that train.

LAURA. It's hot so how about eatin' on that there terrace?

STACY. Sounds great.

LAURA. I found this tablecloth. Kind of colorful. It will perk up the evenin'

GREG. It has perk enough already.

LAURA. (*As GERTA is heard moaning.*) There's somethin' out there.

MATT. (*Goes to L. of sofa.*) It's just a guest relaxing.

LAURA. But she's under a tree and she's moanin'. Is she sick?

MATT. Only if we're lucky.

STACY. I think she is chanting, Laura. It makes her feel good.

LAURA. Everyone to his own taste as the old lady said when she kissed the cow.

STACY. I'm going to stitch that into a sampler.

GREG. (*Rises.*) Laura, would you ask the young lady to step in here, please. I have an idea.

LAURA. If you want. I hope I can get through to her. (*Exits and yells.*) Hey, get yourself in here.

MATT. I think she got through.

STACY. (*TO GREG.*) You've thought of something clever, haven't you?

GREG. Possibly. No, probably.

MATT. What is it?

GREG. (*Goes L. as he thinks it out.*) How did this Gerta person suddenly appear? How did she know we would be here?

STACY. Or, more important, how did she know you would be here?

GREG. Precisely.

MATT. (*Goes to him.*) Mr. B. must have sent her.

STACY. But she has been coming into the office.

GREG. To set up an alibi for this trip?

STACY. Could be.

GREG. Then she is the hit man, I have won the bet. (*Starts U.C. below MATT.*) Let's go home.

MATT. Nonsense. You haven't proved it's her.

GERTA. (*Appears at windows with script in hand. LAURA is behind her.*) You have said, "The moment is now"? I wasn't sure you would know the proper time.

LAURA. (*Glances at her wristwatch as she crosses to dining room.*) The proper time is 8:32. My Timex is never wrong. (*Exits.*)

GREG. Before we start, let me ask you something.

GERTA. (*Marches to him obediently.*) Anything.

GREG. How did you know I was here in this place?

GERTA. I have a friend -

MATT. (*As he sits on the bench.*) I'm surprised.

GERTA. He is a magnificent poet as yet unrecognized.

MATT. He is ahead of his time?

GERTA. You know his work?

MATT. I was joking.

GERTA. (*Patronizingly.*) I should have known. Like me he has never been published so he is forced to work. He has a position with your answering service. He gave me the phone number and the rest was easy.

GREG. We are to assume you also have a friend with the telephone company?

GERTA. A fellow author who is translating life into the Dead Sea Scrolls.

STACY. Answer me one question.

GERTA. (*Moves to windows.*) The question, always the question. Everyone wants an answer to the question. (*Turns and holds her script aloft.*) The answer is in here.

STACY. Then you are not auditioning for anything, you are for real?

GERTA. I am what I am. And now I am outside. It is not right for me to read this now, Mr. Larson. The air is full of hostility.

GREG. Perhaps a bit later.

GERTA. I am patient. If the end comes before you read this, so be it. We never know when the end will be the beginning, do we? (*She smiles tolerantly.*) No, of course we don't. *(Exits.)*

STACY. (*Goes U.C. to GREG.*) Well, we have one suspect on either side of us. (*Gestures in both directions.*)

GREG. At least there's only two. Can't we tie them both up?

MATT. Maybe the real one hasn't gotten here yet. After all, Mr. B. hired some as cover-ups and some, I guess, are real.

STACY. Like Laura, the cook.

GREG. And the irrelevant one with the book must be genuine.

STACY. Let's not let anyone else in. You get those doors and I'll get the front door.

(GREG goes below sofa to the windows and STACY heads for the front door and bumps into BURTON FINLEY. He is a friendly soul of about middle age and is dressed in white overalls and carries a metal tool box. STACY gives a startled scream.)

BURTON. Plumber. Door was open.

MATT. (*Rises.*) We didn't call a plumber.

BURTON. Someone did. I was told what to do. (*Puts his hand into his inside pocket terrifying the others.*)

GREG. (*Takes a step in.*) Don't do that!

BURTON. What?

GREG. Keep your hands where we can see them

BURTON. I'm just showin' you my work order.

GREG. Slowly then.

BURTON. (*Slowly puts his hand inside and pulls out a work order.*) You must be city folks. (*Goes to GREG.*)

MATT. Yes, suspicious city folks.

BURTON. (*Shows him the order.*) See here. "Emergency. Check upstairs bathtub leak."

GREG. We just wanted to make sure.

BURTON. I know what I'm here to do. I'll show you. (*Puts tool box on sofa and unsnaps it.*)

STACY. (*Comes down.*) No! It's a gun!

GREG. (*At same time.*) Stop!

MATT. (*Ducks down by chair C..*) Everyone take cover.

BURTON. (*Pulls out a wrench.*) It's just my wrench.

GREG. Oh, your wrench.

MATT. (*Gets up.*) A wrench? Of course, what a nice wrench. A real beauty.

BURTON. It's just a plain wrench.

GREG. I guess the caretaker called you about the leak?

BURTON. Someone did. Don't know who. (*Snaps box shut.*) I'm surprised you city folks is so nervous. (*Goes to the foot of stairs.*) Ones come up here usually calm as cucumbers. You know what they say does it? Valium.

MATT. You go ahead and fix the leak.

BURTON. You may not have valium but you fellas sure have the prettiest woman.

STACY. Why, thank you.

BURTON. You married to one of them?
STACY. I'm just a secretary.
BURTON. (*With a wicked laugh.*) Oh, sure.
GREG. She is.
STACY. I am.
MATT. That's right.
BURTON. And this sure does look. like an office. Do I see a computer? A file cabinet? One of them fax machines? No, but what I do see is one damn pretty lady. Don't worry, we plumbers take an oath of silence like doctors and lawyers. (*Laughs.*) Secretary? That's what they all say. (*Goes upstairs.*)

STACY. My reputation is in tatters. I deserve a raise.

MATT. (*Sits on the bench.*) Don't you think it a little odd for a plumber to come out on a Saturday night just for a dripping faucet?

STACY. One wrench does not a plumber make.

GREG. I'm going to make a drink. Anyone else?

MATT. Me.

STACY. I'm abstaining but I'll get them for you jet-setters.

GREG. I'll do it. Yours are too weak. And this will give Matt a chance to have you alone for one minute. (*Goes D.L..*) Bar's through here?

STACY. Straight ahead. You can't miss it. (*He exits.*)

MATT. (*Goes to STACY.*) I have one minute alone with you. *(His arms go around her.)*

STACY. There is a killer here somewhere and you get romantic. James Bond you are not.

MATT. I have to make the most of whenever Greg lets you out of his sight.

STACY. (*Pats him and breaks away below desk.*) You do very well on all our dates.

MATT. But you spend most of the time talking about Greg.

STACY. I give you equal time when he takes me out.

MATT. You do like me better than you do him, don't you?

STACY. (*Raises her hand.*) I plead the fifth.

MATT. You'll have to make up your mind between us soon.

STACY. (*Leans back on sofa.*) Fight over me. I love it.

MATT. Do we have a duel at dawn?

STACY. Neither of you could even get up by dawn.

MATT. But we could stay up until then.

STACY. You are both incorrigible and I adore you both.

(PHONE rings.)

GREG. (*Comes in with two highballs.*) Get that, Stacy. (*Stacy goes L. of desk and picks up the phone.*) Here we are. (*Hands drink to MATT.*) Is it too weak?

STACY. (*Into phone.*) Hello ... just a minute, please -

MATT. (*During above.*) Probably, the way you mix them.

STACY. Matt, it's your answering service.

MATT. Take the message will you. (*To GREG.*) Too weak. (*Takes GREG'S glass and drinks .*)

STACY. (*During above, grabs pencil and pad from desk. Into phone.*) This is Mr. Stoddard's secretary. I'll take the message.

GREG. (*During above, to MATT.*) That is mine.

MATT. (*After drinking.*) Yes, this is better.

I BET YOUR LIFE

GREG. They're exactly the same.

STACY. (*Into phone.*) No ... no ... (*To MATT.*) Come here. (*Into phone.*) Would you repeat the message, please.

MATT. (*Takes phone from her and STACY goes to GREG.*) This is Mr. Stoddard.

STACY. Oh, Greg, we'll stop it. We won't let it happen.

GREG. What's going on?

STACY. I don't believe it.

GREG. Neither will I when I hear it. (*MATT hangs up phone in a stupor and looks at GREG.*) Speak.

MATT. The best laid plans and so forth.

GREG. Will someone tell me what it is.

MATT. (*Holds up phone pad on which STACY took down the message.*) I can't read shorthand.

STACY. (*Takes pad from him.*) Listen. "I was on car phone when accident occurred. Plans will proceed without a hitch. Everyone alerted. Have money ready." The caller left no name. (*Sits in chair C.*)

GREG. Not even a "you-know-who"?

LAURA. (*Enters from dining room with napkins and a bud vase with one flower in it .*) The face is passin' through again. Napkins. (*Holds them up.*) Pretty ain't they?

STACY. Very decorative.

LAURA. (*Heads for the windows going below GREG.*) And this flower for the centerpiece.

GREG. (*Goes to her.*) Laura, there is a plumber upstairs.

LAURA. Well, it ain't Corey.

MATT. Who is Corey?

GREG. Obviously the plumber, you idiot.

LAURA. Corey's home with the doc waitin' for Millie to give birth.

MATT. I hope it's a boy.

LAURA. I hope it's a cow. He's got enough bulls.

STACY. (*At foot of stairs.*) If Corey is home, than who is upstairs?

LAURA. Must be some new fella I don't know.

GREG. (*Skeptical.*) Uh-uh.

BURTON. (*Comes downstairs.*) Sorry to interrupt but I forgot somethin'. (*Goes out below STACY and out to front door.*)

LAURA. (*After watching him go.*) That the fella?

GREG. Yes.

LAURA. Don't look like no plumber to me. Clothes is too clean, but then maybe it's his first job.

STACY. You don't know him?

LAURA. Nope.

GREG. You're sure it's nope?

LAURA. Yep. (*Exits out windows.*)

GREG. (*Goes to closet.*) I am going to hide. (*Goes into it.*)

STACY. (*Goes U.C.*) Greg, you had better hide.

GREG. (*Goes by closet.*) I am not going to hide.

MATT. (*Crosses below STACY to closet and opens door.*) If he forgot something it might be his gun.

GREG. I am going to hide. (*Into closet and closes door.*)

MATT. (*Leans casually against the door.*) I hope he's safe in there.

STACY. Bullets can go through doors, you know.

MATT. Don't tell Greg that.

GREG. (*From inside closet.*) I heard.

BURTON. (*Comes in.*) I got it!

STACY. What?

BURTON. (*Holding up instruction book.*) My manual. That's a gosh-darn complicated faucet you got up there.

MATT. You worked around here long?
BURTON. (*Nervously.*) Not long.
MATT. How long?
BURTON. Oops, I hear that faucet leakin'. (*As he runs upstairs.*) Gotta save water these days.
STACY. (*By foot of stairs.*) Strange man. Cute though. I wonder if he's married?
MATT. I'm not married.
GREG. (*Comes out of closet.*) Neither am I.
STACY. (*Goes L. of desk.*) I have a smorgasbord of eligible men.
MATT. Shouldn't Laura and the plumber know each other if they're both local?
GREG. He's new and maybe she - (*Goes to desk..*) Let's look her up in the phone book.
STACY. (*Gets book from desk drawer and sits at desk.*) And I thought Matt was the idea man.
MATT. (*Goes to GREG.*) This evening is my idea. Isn't that enough?
GREG. You overdid it.
STACY. (*Having looked through book.*) ... nine, ten, eleven ...
GREG. What are you doing?
STACY. They must have founded the town.
LAURA. (*Enters from the terrace.*) I have done my best on short notice but that one under the tree asks for things out of season.
STACY. What things?
LAURA. Says she'll eat if I have bean sprouts. (*Moves C..*) Well, beans was planted in May and they're past sproutin'. Why eat a sprout anyway? I say, wait for the whole bean.

(DOORBELL RINGS, They all freeze and look at one another.)

LAURA. Ain't that the doorbell?
ALL THREE. Yes.
LAURA. Am I supposed to answer it?
STACY. *(To MATT.)* Is she?
MATT. *(To GREG.)* Is she?
GREG. *(To LAURA.)* Are you?
LAURA. It won't kill me. *(Goes to front door.)*
GREG. But it might kill me.
LILA. *(Off stage.)* Thank God someone's here.
LAURA. *(Of stage.)* Are you invited?

LILA.(Sails in and leans dramatically against the closet wall. LILA is beyond being an ingenue but doesn't realize it yet. She is very smartly dressed and speaks in a dramatic voice which demands the attention she wants.)

LILA. I am so embarrassed.
MATT. Why?
LILA. I'm having a problem with gas.
STACY. *(Taking an instant dislike to her .)* Personally?
LILA. *(Moves above chair C.)* No, dear, my car. How silly of me not to check my gauge before heading into this desolate countryside. *(LAURA moves in behind LILA.)*
GREG. We're soul-mates.
LAURA. You stayin' for food or not?
LILA. Well, I hardly think I -
MATT. You might as well.
LAURA. She will. *(Goes into dining room.)*

I BET YOUR LIFE

STACY. Can I call a gas station for you or perhaps you are AA?

LILA. Don't you mean AA<u>A</u>?

STACY. Oh, my mistake.

MATT. I have a full tank. Perhaps I can siphon some out for you.

LILA. Let's wait till after I have your generous snack. (*Sits making herself at home in the chair C.*) I am starved and I'm in no great rush.

STACY. So it seems.

LILA. I just had to get away from the city for a few days and there's this charming little inn upstate of here. The pressures, you know.

STACY. Pressures from what?

LILA. Oh. I assumed you recognized me.

STACY. Golly, no.

LILA. I'm an actress. I'm currently on a soap opera.

GREG. (*Looking at MATT.*) But he writes -

MATT. (*Drowning him out, goes to LILA.*) What an interesting life it must be.

LILA. Interesting, yes, and hard but so rewarding.

STACY. (*Goes to foot of stairs.*) I bet you'd like to wash up. (*With a smile.*) You look a fright.

LILA. (*Upset, she rises.*) Do I?

STACY. Let me show you the little girls' room.

LILA. (*Goes to STACY.*) How sweet of you. (*To others.*) Oh, I am Lila Langforth. Perhaps the name - ?

STACY. And I am Stacy Kingsley. Perhaps the name - ? (*A pause while the men exchange a smile and LILA shakes her head.*) I am secretary to Gregory Larson over there.

GREG. Hello.

STACY. And this is a friend, Matthew Stoddard.

MATT. How do.
LILA. A pleasure.
STACY. Come along. (*LILA goes upstairs first.*) You'll run into a plumber and I'm sure he will recognize you. (*They are off.*)
MATT. (*Laughs and sits in chair C.*) Don't you love it when women hate each other on sight?
GREG. (*Crosses to stairs and looks up them.*) She's no soap actress. Your name didn't ring a bell. She didn't ask for a job.
MATT. That out of gas bit went out years ago.
GREG. (*Goes above sofa.*) Stacy said you used it last weekend driving back from the tennis in Forest Hills.
MATT. Just a joke.
GREG. (*Goes to windows.*) Didn't get away with it, did you?
MATT. No more than you did with that "the elevator in my building is broken so perhaps I can stay at your place" routine.
GREG. It did break Tuesday.
MATT. That was Wednesday.
GREG. Don't quibble.
HENRIETTA. (*There is a moan from outside and then she speaks .*) Yoo-hoo. Hello there.
MATT. Now who?
HENRIETTA. (*Off stage.*) Excuse me, little girl, do you live here?
GERTA. (*Off stage.*) I live in the world.
HENRIETTA. (*Off stage.*) How nice.
MATT. You better see who it is. (*DOORBELL rings.*)
GREG. Who's that?

LAURA. (*Off stage in the kitchen*.) I'm not answerin'. I'm washin' lettuce.

MATT. (*Indicating windows*.) You take that one and I'll get the door. (He goes out U.C.)

GREG. (*As he goes out windows*.) Did someone call?

HENRIETTA. (*Off stage*.) I did. Do you live in the world, too?

MATT. (*Off stage*.) Hello.

IRA. (*Off stage*.) What a delightful surprise your invitation was.

MATT. (*Off stage during above*.) It's an evening of surprises.

GREG. *(As he brings in HENRIETTA SQUIRES at same time as MATT brings in IRA WATSON. HENRIETTA is a happy, round, folksy woman wearing a neat dress and carrying a large purse. IRA is a retired businessman and a jovial type.)*

GREG. Won't you come in.

HENRIETTA. Thank you so much.

MATT. Well, here we are. (*They all come at the same time, HENRIETTA ahead of GREG and IRA to the R. of MATT.*)

IRA. Hello everyone.

HENRIETTA. Isn't this delightful?

IRA. (*Goes down be HENRIETTA..*) I'm Ira Watson. I live down the road. (*Points.*)

HENRIETTA. And I'm Henrietta Squires and I, too, live down the road. (*Points in same direction.*)

IRA. But the other way, I guess.

HENRIETTA. Yes, that's right. (*Quickly points the opposite way.*)

GREG. (*Goes by bench.*) I am Gregory Larson and this is Matthew Stoddard.

HENRIETTA. Delighted.

MATT. You mean you two are neighbors and you don't know each other?

IRA AND HENRIETTA. I just moved - (*They stop and laugh.*)

IRA. What a coincidence.

GREG. Yes.

HENRIETTA. I'd hardly moved in when I got your invite to stop by. So neighborly.

IRA. Same here. So neighborly.

STACY. (*Has come downstairs during above.*) Well, well, people do drop in.

GREG. Stacy Kingsley, this is Henrietta -?

HENRIETTA. Squires.

GREG. And Ira Watson.

STACY. (*Comes down.*) How nice to meet you.

MATT. They're neighbors.

GREG. But they don't know each other.

STACY. (*With a knowing look.*) Oh!

HENRIETTA. Miss Kingsley, there is a strange female sitting out there cross-legged and she is humming.

STACY. She's an author.

HENRIETTA. I thought maybe this was some kind of rehabilitation center.

STACY. It's turning into one.

LILA. (*Comes downstairs followed by BURTON*). This nice gentleman has offered to siphon his tank, too.

BURTON. My pleasure.

LILA. I'm sorry. Am I interrupting?

MATT. We're just going outside to the terrace for a bite of supper.

GREG. You too, Burton.

BURTON. That's real nice of you.

LILA. (*As the guests go on to the terrace.*) I am Lila Langforth but then I expect you know that.

HENRIETTA. Of course, didn't we meet at the general store?

LILA. (*Frostily.*) I believe not.

BURTON. This lady's a TV star.

IRA. Isn't that exciting.

LILA. (*As they disappear.*) For you, I'm sure.

STACY. (*Goes out and calls down to GERTA.*) Gerta, why not join us? I'm sure we have something for you.

GERTA. (*Off stage.*) Tofu and tiger's milk will do.

STACY. (*Comes back in.*) How does one milk a tiger?

MATT. Under anesthesia. (*STACY goes above sofa to desk.*)

GREG. Have you noticed that none of them is connected? Any one of them could be the hit man.

LAURA. (*Enters with a tray of silverware and crosses to windows.*) I'm puttin' out the knives and forks. How many we got now?

MATT. Four plus that odd one if she decides to join in.

LAURA. (*Looks out windows.*) She's comin'. Looks hungry enough.

LILA. (*Off stage.*) Yes, dear people, it's true. I am Lila Langforth.

LAURA. (*As she exits.*) Yes, dear people, it is true, here comes Laura Pudney.

GREG. There they all are and not one of them can prove who he or she is.

MATT. (*To STACY who is on the phone.*) Who are you calling?

STACY. (*Into phone.*) Operator, this is an emergency. Get me the nearest hospital. (*To others.*) Time is running out.

MATT. When Mr. B. regains consciousness he can tell the hit man to call it off. This is getting out of control.

STACY. (*Into phone.*) Yes ... I am calling about a car accident that happened just below our house and our friends ... yes, thank you. (*To others as GREG crosses in.*) She's connecting me to the emergency room.

GREG. You are resourceful, isn't she, Matt?

MATT. Extremely.

STACY. (*Into phone.*) Yes, the accident ... please ... you're sure? ... thank you. (*Hangs up.*)

MATT AND GREG. Well?

STACY. The driver and the passenger are both deceased.

CURTAIN

ACT II

(A short time later. The glasses have been cleared. From occasional sounds it is clear the guests are on the terrace and GREG enters from there and goes to the phone, dials 911.)

GREG. *(Into phone.)* 911? ... How do I reach the police, the sheriff, whoever you have out here? ... of course, it's an emergency. There has never been a more urgent emergency since Paul Revere rode through here ... tell me how I can get the sheriff before I am snuffed ... no, not that kind of snuff. I am not on anything ... please get me the sheriff ... if he's not in then where is he? ... Can I have a number where he is? ... *(Writes it down on a pad.)* Thank you very much, you have just saved a valuable life. *(Hangs up.)* I shall never leave the city again. I shall never even go into Central Park after dark. That's silly. No one ever goes into Central Park after dark.

STACY. *(Has come in during above and comes up behind him)* Gregory.

GREG. *(Jumps.)* Don't do that.

STACY. Do what?

GREG. Try to scare me to death.

STACY. Do you think you ought to be alone?

GREG. Everyone else is out there.

STACY. Except Laura Pudney.

GREG. That's right.

STACY. And where is the plumber?

GREG. He's taking his things out to the car.

STACY. He could be bringing in an elephant gun for all you know.

GREG. His wrench was enough of a lethal weapon.

STACY. If we can just get Burton-the-plumber out there with everyone else you'll be safe.

GREG. Laura goes back and forth like a Swiss barometer.

STACY. She could be a killer. Kathleen Turner was one in PRIZZI'S HONOR.

GREG. I remember.

STACY. And what about Ma Barker?

GREG. And Lady Macbeth and Bonnie even without Clyde.

STACY. That's enough.

GREG. (*Moves away D.R.*) Damn Matthew Stoddard anyway.

STACY. Why? He's trying to prove a point, isn't he? He is showing you that his script is possible and besides you love a good bet.

GREG. Depends on the prize.

STACY. (*Sits in chair C..*) I admit this is going a bit far but let's concentrate on the person.

GREG. (*Goes to windows.*) I can't stand on the terrace and suddenly say, "Whoever you are, the deal is off."

STACY. But you can act like a man who doesn't want to be shot.

GREG. (*Turns to her.*) What more can I do, tell everyone. I have booked passage on a world cruise on the QE3 whenever it is built?

STACY. If you just looked a bit healthier.

GREG. I am the picture of health. Aren't I like one of those ads for Nordic-Track?

STACY. Not quite. You do look a bit terminal.

GREG. That's the strain of tonight.

STACY. You must impress everyone how healthy you are and so whoever it is will realize this is all a mistake.

GREG. Or maybe I could pay him off. That would be a new twist, pay someone not to shoot you. This could become very popular. It could replace asking for extra change. They could simply say, "One hundred bucks or you're dead meat!"

STACY. Sure, get a receipt and have a deductible expense.

GREG. *(Sits on sofa.)* Now you're trying to be funny.

STACY. Do you honestly think one of those people out there is a hit person?

GREG. Don't you?

STACY. Matt does seem terribly worried, doesn't he?

GREG. He must be. He's not that good an actor to be putting it on.

STACY. He's holding his own on the terrace but how long can he keep up that friendly banter?

GREG. Banter is a soap writer's specialty. He's studying for his next script.

STACY. *(Rises and goes to sofa.)* What we have to do is find out who is the hit person and disarm him.

GREG. Or her.

STACY. *(Perches on sofa arm by him.)* I mean disarm as in "mentally call it off" not physically remove the gun. You couldn't do that.

GREG. So I am not an ad for Nordic-Track, but I have been clever. *(Rises, goes to desk and holds up pad.)* I called 911 and I got the number where the sheriff is. If we could reach him he could round up a posse or send a chopper or something dramatic.

STACY. *(Goes to L. of desk.)* No harm in calling him.

GREG. Maybe they have a photo file on hit people and he can bring it over and we can match it up and then go back to the city.

STACY. (*She picks up the phone.*) What's the number?

GREG. (*Reads it from the pad.*) 834-2424.

STACY. (*Dials.*) These country sheriffs are so clever.

GREG. (*Sits on the bench.*) I never thought standard clothing for the country would be a bullet proof vest.

STACY. Number's busy. (*Hangs up.*)

GREG. Crime runs rampant in the woods.

LAURA. (*Comes in from kitchen with tray of egg rolls.*) You better get on the terrace, finger food is on the way.

STACY. Looks tasty.

LAURA. (*Goes to windows.*) Don't know myself. When I eat I really eat, none of this little stuff.

GREG. What are they?

LAURA. This here is frozen Chinese egg rolls.

STACY. Delicious.

LAURA. I microwaved them. Hope I don't get cancer.

GREG. (*Gets an idea and goes to LAURA.*) I ate in a Chinese restaurant last night and guess what the fortune cookie said?

STACY. But we ate in -

GREG. (*Drowning her out.*) It said, "You have a long life. Any one who shortens it for you will face a horrible death."

STACY. (*Gets it.*) Oh.

LAURA. You must eat in peculiar restaurants. All fortune cookies I've seen have good news.

GREG. It sure doesn't make it sound good for anyone who would wish me dead, does it?

LAURA. Why would anyone want you dead? You seem harmless.

GREG. I am, completely.

Laura. You don't do anything mean to the environment, do you?

GREG. No, nothing at all. I recycle, I don't smoke, I don't use styrofoam cups, I have even donated my organs for transplants.

STACY. (*Moves in below bench.*) Gregory -

GREG. No, I shouldn't have said that.

STACY. No, you shouldn't.

GREG. I mean my organs are donated only if I die of old age.

STACY. Yes, over eighty.

GREG. So I have to wait a long time to pass on or no one can have my valuable parts.

LAURA. Don't know how valuable they will be by then.

GREG. Research. Yes, for research.

LAURA. If I was you, I'd go back to that Chinese place and get a different cookie. (*Exits.*)

STACY. That cookie bit was very clever.

GREG. (*Goes to her.*) Wasn't it though?

STACY. It got you nowhere but it was very clever.

GREG. She wouldn't kill me and ruin an organ donation, would she?

STACY. If she's a hired gun, I don't think a heart and a liver would make much difference. (*Goes to L. of desk.*) I'll call the sheriff again.

GREG. (*Gets pad as she picks up phone.*) 834-2424.

STACY. (*Dials.*) Maybe the sheriff is investigating the car accident or he's at the hospital.

GREG. Why did Mr. B. have to go out and get killed tonight?

STACY. (*Hangs up and glances down at pad.*) Damn, busy again.

GREG. Do sheriffs get days off?

STACY. (*With extreme patience.*) Gregory -

GREG. When you use that tone I know I have done something stupid.

STACY. This phone number you gave me -

GREG. Yes.

STACY. It is this phone. I have been dialing myself.

GREG. Then that means the sheriff is here somewhere.

STACY. Precisely.

GREG. Do you think it could be Laura of the egg rolls?

STACY. Or? (*Looks toward front door.*)

GREG. Who?

STACY. Our friendly plumber?

GREG. (*Goes below sofa.*) The real sheriff could be out there lying under a rhododendron. Let's give him the third degree when he comes in.

STACY. (*Goes above desk.*) Right.

GREG. (*When she is U.C..*) Don't they always grill suspects under a bare bulb?

STACY. Let's be less dramatic and more civilized. (*They both look towards front door.*) Where is he?

GREG. He's flown the coop.

STACY. Your language has gotten very countrified.

LILA. (*Enters from terrace.*) Excuse me.

GREG. (*As they both turn to her.*) Oh, it's you.

LILA. Yes I think so.

GREG. (*Comes down.*) Is the plumber out there?

LILA. No. Why should he be? There are no faucets dripping on the terrace.

STACY. (*Goes above desk.*) We want to be sure he doesn't leave before supper.

LILA. How democratic.

GREG. Did you want something special in here?

LILA. That person - your cook - I don't drink just any water and I asked for some Evian.

STACY. And she said?

LILA. To quote her, "What we got's in the fridge."

STACY. I'm sure the water here is good and pure.

LILA. For you perhaps, my dear, but I have to be so careful. My career, you know. And where is this fridge?

STACY. (*Crosses by bench.*) I assume in the kitchen.

LILA. How clever of you. And where is the kitchen?

GREG. (*Goes D.L. to arch.*) Right through here. The house is supposed to be well stocked so I am sure we have some kind of water.

LILA. Thank you, Mr. Larson. I am sure you know how important good health is for a good body and you must admit my body is good. (*She has crossed very close to him.*)

GREG. It's -

STACY. The fridge is through there.

LILA. It is said that one's body is one's temple. (*Exits.*)

STACY. (*Looking after her.*) I think that temple is decaying like the Acropolis.

GREG. But like the Acropolis it's a nice thing to visit.

MATT. (*Comes in from terrace.*) What are you doing in here? The party is outside.

GREG. We are trying to stay alive.

STACY. He means the royal "we" not both of us.

MATT. If you don't find the hit person soon I win my bet.

GREG. (*Moves in.*) Over my dead body.

MATT. I hope not. I really hope not.

GREG. I'm so glad you're amused.

MATT. Those two supposed neighbors out there do not know each other and each claims to have just moved here. Coincidence? I doubt it. Why are they lying?

STACY. Not only that but Burton-the-plumber may be the sheriff.

MATT. (*Sits on sofa.*) How did you find that out?

GREG. Intelligence.

MATT. That means Stacy did something.

STACY. Right. (*Goes to windows.*) Suppose I go out and entertain for a bit. I may get some more information.

GREG. (*Sits in chair C..*) I'll stay here and be less of a target.

MATT. It's not ten o'clock yet.

BURTON. (*Enters from front door and dressed in slacks and a sport shirt.*) Here I am all spruced up and ready for the feed bag.

GREG. So colloquial.

BURTON. I always keep a change of clothes in the truck. You never know.

STACY. Why not come out here with me, Burton. May I call you Burton?

BURTON. Why not?

STACY. Or would you rather be called sheriff?

BURTON. (*Goes above sofa to her.*) No, my name's Finley, Burton Finley. You forgot.

STACY. I am confused. I thought someone called you sheriff and I thought it was your last name unless, of course, you are the sheriff.

BURTON. (*Confused.*) Well now, little lady, I just could be that, you know, but for the evening I am just Burton-the-plumber. Let's eat.

STACY. (*A backward glance as they exit.*) I just bet you are the sheriff. You look the type.

BURTON. Rugged and prepared for anything, right? That's me.

STACY. You look like an ad for Nordic-Track. (*They are off.*)

GREG. He doesn't seem to know he's the sheriff either.

MATT. My money's on the soap actress.

GREG. Lila Langforth?

MATT. If she works so much then how come she doesn't recognize my name? Those actresses are always after us writers.

LILA. (*Comes in from dining room with a glass of Evian water.*) But I do know your name, darling. Of course I do. Everyone does, but I didn't want to push myself the way those eager-beaver ingenues do.

MATT. Really?

LILA. (*Moves below sofa and very close to him.*) You might think I knew you would be here and pretended to have my car run out of gas, but, no, no, no it was a true mistake but then Freud says there are no mistakes so here I am and here you are.

MATT. Yes.

GREG. And me, too. I am here.

LILA. Of course you are. (*With a long and odd look at him.*) I know you are here.

MATT. (*Rises.*) And you want to know what's going to happen on my soap when Maxine comes out of her coma. Every housewife in the U.S. is wondering.

LILA. And me, too, darling, wondering and wondering. But I know you. You have a surprise up your computer. I'll have to wait along with everyone else to hear Maxine's fate. (*Goes to windows.*) But I cannot wait for one of those tiny egg rolls. I hope they're fat free. Oh, the hell with my diet. (*Exits.*)

GREG. (*Rises and goes to MATT.*) What was that all about? Maxine is not in a coma.

MATT. That is the point. Maxine got married to Richard last week. It was our best ratings of the year.

GREG. So Lila is not an actress?

MATT. Actress, possibly, but certainly not on daytime.

GREG. Do you suppose she's got a hand gun stuck in her garter?

MATT. Didn't you notice? She wasn't wearing a garter.

GREG. You are observant.

LAURA. (*Comes in from terrace holding empty tray.*) Dead!

GREG. What is?

LAURA. This tray of egg rolls. They sure is hungry guests. (*Starts for kitchen.*) That one who calls everyone darling, she put a whole handful on her napkin. All that fuss over some bottled water and then she gobbles that junk.

MATT. (*Goes D.C..*) How about the other two? Do they seem happy?

LAURA. Sure do. They're gettin' along right well. I think he's comin' on to her, you know what I mean?

GREG. That even happens in the city.

LAURA. But I'm not too sure about them not knowing each other before.

MATT. Why?

LAURA. Oh, little things, sort of private things they laugh at together and the way they look at each other. They could be up to something, maybe casing the house for a burglary. That happens, you know, when houses is closed up in the country.

GREG. (*Crossed in C.*) Maybe we should alert the sheriff.

LAURA. Nope.

GREG. Why not?

LAURA. Sheriff's off this week attendin' a meetin' on crime prevention..

MATT. Really?

LAURA. In Colorado.

GREG. Then there is no sheriff?

LAURA. Not till Monday next. We got some deputies though. I gotta bring in the salad now.

GREG. What kind?

LAURA. I decided on what they call Chef's Salad. I just went down to my friends steak house and gave him a few bucks and scooped up at his salad bar. Now I'll throw some of them croutons on top and sprinkle some paprika and who'll know the diff? Your friends will love it.

GREG. Probably.

LAURA. Forgot them ain't your friends and they're not each other's friends neither except those two neighbors. Odd bunch. (*Exits.*)

GREG. That one seems genuine all right.

MATT. They all seem genuine.

GREG. Does Mr. B. go through a casting agent or what?

MATT. Even Burton could be a real deputy.

GREG. (*Turns to windows.*) Maybe we can spot the one who is overacting.

MATT. Like which?

GREG. (*There is a moan and GERTA comes through the windows.*). Like this.

GERTA. (*Carries the script.*) The moon is high. The time is now.

GREG. (*Backs up and sits on the sofa.*) It's not ten o'clock.

GERTA. Somewhere in the world it is ten 'clock. Somewhere in the world it is tomorrow and somewhere yesterday, but here it is today. Are you ready?

GREG. For what?

GERTA. For what you are about to receive?

GREG. (*Rises just above as GERTA kneels beside him.*) She's the one. I found her. I win the bet.

MATT. Are you sure?

GERTA. (*Opens book and reads.*) "It is the day after tomorrow. The bomb has fallen."

MATT. It is a bomb.

GERTA. "The earth is a wasteland like the brains of the survivors."

GREG. (*To MATT.*) It's not her. This is real.

GERTA. (*Rises.*) I'm glad you realize that. Other agents have merely scoffed.

GREG. Imagine starting a story the day after the bomb falls. Original, isn't it, Matt?

MATT. Never heard of it before.

GERTA. Settle down now and I shall read the entire work. (*Sits on sofa..*)

MATT. We only have the house for the weekend.

GREG. (*Goes below her and lifts her up guiding her to the windows.*) I have to think, my dear. I have to think hard. This opening has struck a chord inside me. Go, go sit again under that tree. Go collect your thoughts as I shall collect mine. Go, go and chant as you have never chanted before. Go. (*Pushes her out.*)

GERTA. I go. (*She does.*)

GREG. She is gone.

MATT. (*Sits on bench.*) She is very far gone.

GREG. (*Goes D.C..*) I am crossing her off my list unless she intends to smother me to death with verbs and dangling participles.

MATT. I wrote a line like that last week. Richard said it to Mona.

GREG. I know.

STACY. (*Enters while glancing back.*) You're still alive?

MATT. Gerta is not.

STACY. So let's do what Sherlock Holmes does.

GREG. What?

STACY. Eliminate everything else until there is only one possibility left.

MATT. Which is?

STACY. One of the others out there.

LAURA. (*Comes rushing in with deep wooden salad bowl covered with a tea towel.*) Gangway!

STACY. (*As LAURA rushes through and out windows.*) There goes one of the others.

GREG. If we have crossed off the cook, the existentialist author, how about the neighbors who don't know each other?

STACY. (*Crosses in.*) Let's prove to them how healthy you are and then they will know there has been a mistake.

GREG. A big mistake.

STACY. I have an idea. Matt, send in Ira Watson.

MATT. *(Rises.)* In the middle of his salad?

STACY. Go on.

MATT. *(Goes out to the terrace.)* He can go to Pizza Hut later.

STACY. *(Takes GREG to the closet.)* Now you get into that closet.

GREG. What for?

STACY. I am going to prove to him how healthy you are. Go on. *(Opens door and starts to push him in.)*

GREG. But I don't want to go in there.

STACY. Get in that closet. *(Pushes him in as LAURA runs through from terrace to dining room.)*

LAURA. *(Stops dead midway.)* You playin' hide and seek or what?

STACY. Just checking the hinges on the door.

GREG. They squeak, need oil.

LAURA. All I got's Wesson oil and it's all on the salad. *(Rushes off.)*

STACY. Go on, Greg. I am going to act.

GREG. But - *(She closes the door and turns away as it starts to open again, she shuts it and there is an "Ow" from GREG inside.)*

STACY. Sorry. *(Rushes to phone and picks it up with an eye on the windows. Speaks on phone when she sees IRA coming in. He has a napkin tucked in his collar.)* Thank you, doctor ... you're sure? ... You're positive, doctor? ... a very long life? Very good, doctor ... Thank you, doctor. *(Hangs up, turns and sees IRA.)* Oh!

IRA. I didn't mean to interrupt.

STACY. That was the doctor.

IRA. So I gathered.

STACY. I guess you did. Well, Greg - Mr. Larson - is in fine health.

IRA. That's certainly good news.

STACY. (*Moves U.C..*) Yes, we knew he was healthy but we wanted to make sure. Absolutely sure, and we did.

IRA. I couldn't be happier.

STACY. So there is no reason why he shouldn't live to a ripe old age.

IRA. Good.

STACY. No reason at all. (*Closet door has opened a crack, she slams it and there is another "Ow" from inside.*)

IRA. What was that?

STACY. (*Crosses to C. of sofa.*) Creaking boards. You know these old houses.

IRA. But this one is new.

STACY. New ones are worse. Bad workmanship.

IRA. (*After a pause.*) Are you coming outside to join us for supper?

STACY. Yes, of course. (*Sits on sofa.*) First I wanted to ask you the name of a good doctor in case we need one for Mr. Larson but then I called his own doctor and got this wonderful report, really outstanding report, so I don't need to know anyone local.

IRA. (*Sits beside her.*) I wouldn't know one anyway since I just moved here.

STACY. Of course, that's right. Where did you come from?

IRA. Lately from San Francisco.

STACY. San Quentin.

IRA. Pardon?

STACY. Isn't there a prison there? San Quentin. I saw a Burt Lancaster movie about it.

IRA. I had to stay there for ten years.

STACY. In prison?

IRA. No, in San Francisco. I signed a contract with a building firm. I'm an architect.

Stacy. Oh.

IRA. (*Rises.*) I am also hungry. Shall we join the others?

STACY. Yes, of course.

IRA. (*As they head out windows.*) Very friendly people around here except possibly that odd one under the tree. She asked your cook for organic chamomile tea.

STACY. What did Laura say?

IRA. Said she wasn't making tea out of her bathrobe and Mrs. Squires said that was chenille. (*The closet door has opened as they go off and STACY gives a backward glance and a thumbs up sign. GREG starts to follow them when LAURA rushes in with a covered bread dish and heads for the windows.*)

LAURA. Move it.

GREG. Sorry.

LAURA. Biscuits.

GREG. Good. I was worried about them

LAURA. No problem. Frozen. Pop up kind.

GREG. Good.

LAURA. (*Starts out windows and bumps into MATT.*) Out of the way. Biscuits comin' through. (*Exits.*)

MATT. Everyone's eating up a storm

GREG. (*Comes D.C..*) I have yet to have a bite of the condemned man's last meal.

MATT. How did you make out with that Watson man?

GREG. Stacy impressed him I was as healthy as a horse.

MATT. They shoot horses don't they?

GREG. Not everyone knows I am healthy and not suicidal.

MATT. Everyone except Henrietta Squares, friendly neighbor.

GREG. *(Sits in chair C.)* She's too typical to believe.

MATT. Which may be why she is hired for the job.

GREG. There must be some genuine folksy people or how would we know who to imitate.

MATT. You better check her out.

GREG. How?

MATT. *(Crosses to him.)* That's up to you. I told her you wanted to see her.

GREG. What for?

MATT. That's your problem. I can't do everything for you.

LAURA. *(Comes trotting through to dining room.)* Butter problem!

GREG. You forgot the butter?

LAURA. I did not. Some want it only if it is lite.

GREG. Do we have that?

LAURA. I'll put the same butter on another plate. They'll never know. Tastes the same.

MATT. You want a job at an ad agency?

LAURA. Won't leave the country no way. You city folks have to join clubs to get your exercise. I just serve supper to finicky eaters and I gets all the exercise I need. Just watch me jog out of here. *(She jogs off.)*

MATT. What an idea, wives paying to cook for other people so they won't have to exercise in a gym. There's a plot in there somewhere.

GREG. Drop it.

HENRIETTA. (*Appears in French windows.*) Hello.

MATT. (*Goes below sofa.*) Come in, Mrs. Squires. Gregory here wants to see you.

HENRIETTA . How nice.

MATT. I'll leave you two alone.

GREG. (*Rises.*) You don't have to.

MATT. Yes, I do. (*Exits with a smile.*)

HENRIETTA. Your cook has prepared a delightful salad.

GREG. How nice.

HENRIETTA. But you haven't had any yet.

GREG. No, I - I don't want to embarrass my guests but I can't eat that salad. Too fattening.

HENRIETTA. (*Sits on sofa.*) I don't think so. It looks most healthful to me.

GREG. I had a small plate in here without dressing.

HENRIETTA. I wish I could stick to a diet like that.

GREG. It's all part of my plan. Diet and exercise. (*Glances at this watch.*) Oh-oh, I'm missing my jogging. (*Rises and starts jogging in place between the chair and the desk.*)

HENRIETTA. I swim for exercise but, of course, only in the summer.

GREG. But I am in training.

HENRIETTA. Olympics?

GREG. (*Still jogging up and down.*) No, the Surgeon General is going to use me as an example for all American men.

HENRIETTA. How exciting.

GREG. I am to be photographed every month for display ads in buses and magazines every month for years - (*Stops jogging and is panting .*)

HENRIETTA. Really?

GREG. - and years, way into the future. (*Leans on chair C. barely able to speak.*)

HENRIETTA. That's as long as you jog?

GREG. I did ten miles this morning.

HENRIETTA. Ten miles?

GREG. Yes, driving up here I jogged along the Merritt Parkway while they drove beside me.

HENRIETTA. I trust you were in the slow lane. (*Laughs and he joins her as he collapses in chair C.*)

GREG. I have to stop every few minutes and check my pulse. (*Holds his wrist but with his thumb on the inside.*)

HENRIETTA. (*Rises.*) You're doing it wrong.

GREG. What?

HENRIETTA. (*Takes the index finger and reverses it with his thumb so it is inside of the wrist.*) That's how you do it. I'm a gray lady at the hospital.

GREG. I was so busy talking I got confused.

HENRIETTA. You wanted to see me about something?

GREG. Yes, oh, yes.

HENRIETTA. What?

GREG. A - er - seamstress. Yes, a seamstress. I have a little mending I need done. You must know some local lady who is good with a needle and thread.

HENRIETTA. Well -

LAURA. (*Enters from dining room with covered butter dish and crosses to the L. of GREG.*) Me! I can sew up a storm. Just give me what's to be done after I do the dishes.

HENRIETTA. There we are, problem solved.

LAURA. (*Goes R..*) Gotta get this here butter - this here lite butter - out there before it melts. (*To outsiders as she exits.*) Hold on, lite stuff comin' in.

HENRIETTA. (*After she and GREG exchange a look.*) Quaint.

GREG. But not as quaint as you.

HENRIETTA. What do you mean?

GREG. I'm in show business and I know you are too perfect.

HENRIETTA. (*Sighs as goes to desk.*) Quaint is my profession.

GREG. I suspected. What's your story? Are you in the witness protection program because you squealed on a spy?

HENRIETTA. (*Enjoying this all.*) No, guess again.

GREG. You charm rich old men into marriage for their insurance?

HENRIETTA. I could be working on that Ira Watson right now or even on you.

GREG. Or you could be a hit man.

HENRIETTA. Could be.

GREG. Wouldn't that be clever to have a nice neighborly woman as a hit person?

HENRIETTA. Very clever. (*Opens her rather large purse. It looks ominous to GREG and he rises.*)

GREG. It's not ten o'clock yet.

HENRIETTA. What happens at ten, deep knee bends?

GREG. Suppose you are a hit person.

HENRIETTA. Suppose I am.

GREG. And suppose I give you one thousand dollars not to kill me. What would you do?

HENRIETTA. Are you offering me one thousand dollars not to kill you?

GREG. Yes.

HENRIETTA. I'll take it. (*Pulls hand from purse and it holds a card.*) You may want to keep this on file.

GREG. What is it?

HENRIETTA. My photo and the agency number. I model.

GREG. You do quaint?

HENRIETTA. (*Sits on the bench.*) I am the quaintest, folksiest country woman available.

GREG. Of course. I've seen you on those Corn Flakes.

HENRIETTA. Centrum Silver.

GREG. Shake' n Bake.

HENRIETTA. Don't forget the toilet bowl cleaner.

GREG. Good for you.

HENRIETTA. Now, about that thousand dollars.

GREG. Oh, that.

HENRIETTA. If everyone I meet offers me a thousand dollars not to kill them I could retire and stop being quaint.

GREG. I'll have my secretary, Stacy out there, write out a check for you.

HENRIETTA. Cash, no checks.

GREG. Of course.

HENRIETTA. (*Relaxes, laughs and becomes less folksy.*) You're an author aren't you?

GREG. No, that's Matthew. I'm his agent.

HENRIETTA. Me as a hit man or, what did you say, a hit person? I thought you were testing out a new plot. A thousand dollars indeed.

GREG. But I thought -

HENRIETTA. I've been doing my act all evening.

GREG. What act?

HENRIETTA. The one I use for press conferences. Besides modeling, I write children's books for a living.

GREG. You do?

HENRIETTA. Under the name of Granny Smith.

GREG. (*Sits on chair C..*) Like the apples?

HENRIETTA. The name is familiar and it sells. Grandma Moses started that whole bit and it pays off.

GREG. Of course I've heard of the Granny Smith books.

HENRIETTA. So what was your idea with the thousand dollars?

GREG. Just trying a little improvisation.

LAURA. (*Off stage we hear she and STACY as they approach.*) That just about does it. Salad dressing was one thing, butter was another but this is the end. I quit.

STACY. I'll help you . We can manage.

GREG. (*During above, he rises.*) Now what?

HENRIETTA. I suspect temperament in the kitchen.

LAURA. (*Charges in followed by STACY.*) One dessert, that's all I am hired to do.

STACY. It's just ice cream.

LAURA. (*Goes below sofa to GREG.*) I ask you, Mr. Larson, and you, Miss Whoever -

HENRIETTA. Squires.

LAURA. One dessert I am to supply. One. That doesn't mean three, does it? (*Stacy sinks on to the sofa.*)

GREG. No.

LAURA. Ice cream. That is one dessert, isn't it?

HENRIETTA. That was your mistake dear. They wanted to know what type, didn't they?

LAURA. (*Goes to her.*) Vanilla, chocolate, strawberry, that I could handle.

GREG. So give them one or the other.

LAURA. No, they asked if it is fat free, frozen yogurt, or iced milk.

HENRIETTA. What did you say, dear?

LAURA. I said it's damn plain old ice cream and I made tracks.

STACY. It's a warm night so why don't you just serve it and they can eat it or ignore it.

LAURA. You got horse sense. (*Exits mumbling as she goes into dining room.*) Yogurt, iced milk, fat free, what the hell.

HENRIETTA. (*Rises and goes to windows.*) I'll eat whichever is served. (*Starts out as LILA come in.*)

LILA. I really should be leaving as soon as some gas is siphoned into my car.

HENRIETTA. (*Crosses below her to windows.*) Stick around, dear, and make one thousand dollars. That's what I've done. Miss Kingsley, I'll take a check only if it's made out to cash. (*Exits.*)

LILA. (*Goes to GREG.*) One thousand dollars, what for?

GREG. Just a little joke we have.

LILA. (*Goes closer to him*) I'll do most anything for a thousand dollars.

STACY. I'm sure you would.

GREG. Would you not kill me for that amount?

LILA. You're on.

STACY. This is turning into an expensive evening.

LILA. (*Goes to windows.*) Perhaps I will stay around for ice cream and whatever else happens.

STACY. Please do.

LILA. (*At windows.*) I've changed my mind. You're nice so I will not kill you for seven hundred and fifty dollars. How's that?

GREG. A bargain.

LILA. I'm not sure I understand what is happening here but I think I just made some money. (*Exits.*)

STACY. (*Rises and goes to GREG.*) I don't believe this. You are throwing money away like confetti on New Year's Eve.

GREG. I can't take it with me, can I?

STACY. You could leave it to your secretary.

MATT. (*Rushes in.*) What the hell is going on? Everyone was upset about some kind of ice cream and now they're all talking about how healthy you are.

GREG. I jogged up the Merritt Parkway.

STACY. You slept up the Merritt Parkway.

GREG. (*Goes below her to MATT.*) I think this bet has gone far enough. Let's call it off.

MATT. How can we?

GREG. Tell everyone we know who the hit man is and that we have informed the FBI. Then he or she will quickly disappear.

MATT. You don't identify the hit man you lose the bet and you'll take the script to Hollywood.

GERTA. (*Appears at windows holding the script.*) No!

ALL THREE. (*Turn.*) What?

GERTA. This book will not go to Hollywood.

MATT. Good.

GREG. I agree wholeheartedly.

GERTA. I will not prostitute myself.

STACY. I am not saying a word.

GERTA. When you have read this then (*Holds out script.*) you will understand why I shall turn down even the National Book Award.

GREG. I have other things on my mind right at the moment.

GERTA. The moment? Life is but a moment. This is the time. The time is now. (*Sits on the sofa arm facing in, opens the script and reads.*) "An untitled work by Gerta." No title. No last name. This is the commencing of surprises. "It is the day - "

STACY. (*Signals him.*) Matt, help. (*As MATT helps her lift GERTA to standing.*) The vibes are wrong. Can you not feel them?

GERTA. No, I - I -

STACY. (*As she and MATT guide GERTA to the window.*) They are all around us, the wrong vibes, aren't they, Matthew?

MATT. Yes, vibes. Wrong.

GERTA. Yes, yes now I do feel them. They are surrounding me.

STACY. Go, later come back when your verbs and adjectives are cleansed.

GERTA. (*As she disappears.*) Yes, yes, I knew you would be sensitive. I now know you are the reincarnation of George Sand.

STACY. You got it.

GERTA. (*Off stage.*) Thank you George. (*Gives a few of her moans.*)

GREG. (*To STACY.*) You have hidden talents.

STACY. I am more than a secretary, you know.

GREG. (*Goes to her.*) I have always known.

MATT. (*To her other side.*) As have I.

GREG. Which is why I never look upon you as a secretary when we date.

STACY. (*Smiles.*) I know.

MATT. I only look upon you as an attractive, desirable, wonderful woman.

STACY. (*Smiles.*) I know.

GREG. I think you should stop going out with him and concentrate on me.

STACY. Should I?

MATT. You should enjoy yourself out of the office. He's a sore loser anyway.

GREG. I am not a sore loser.

MATT. I don't see you winning this bet.

GREG. I am now going to take the bull by the horns.

MATT. Your specialty is bull.

GREG. You writers are a bore.

STACY. (*Goes below bench.*) Gentlemen, please, control yourselves.

GREG. I am taking care of everything. (*Calls out windows.*) Hello. Hello, out there. I have an announcement to make.

MATT. (*To STACY.*) What's he up to?

GREG. I am prepared to offer each of you one thousand dollars to leave here peacefully -

(*Cheers and applause from off stage.*)

STACY. That's a fortune.

GREG. (*Calling.*) - and not kill me. (*Murmurs from off stage.*) However, if even one of you declines this offer than none of you can accept the money.

MATT. Clever.

GREG. (*Continues calling.*) Think it over and let me know. I shall be here with my secretary and my checkbook. That is all. Over and out. (*Comes back into room.*)

MATT. You think that's smart, don't you?

GREG. Yes.

MATT. Well, it is but suppose whoever it is takes the money and then shoots you anyway?

GREG. (*Goes below him to C.*) Then Stacy will cancel the checks.

MATT. You don't identify him you lose the bet.

GREG. But I save my life. You wouldn't dare hold me to the bet since it all turned out differently than you planned. (*Looks at him.*) Would you? (*Looks again.*) Yes, you would.

MATT. A triumph for me.

GREG. Anyway it is ten o'clock and I'm still here.

STACY. Maybe the hit is coming on Standard time.

GREG. What time is that?

MATT. I've never been able to figure whether we have to spring ahead or fall behind.

GREG. Who knows?

STACY. I do. (*From the purse on the desk she pulls out a pistol.*) It is ten o'clock somewhere in the world right now.

GREG. What are you doing with that?

MATT. Stacy!

STACY. (*Goes below bench.*) I am setting myself free. I am preparing for my future. I am about to retire somewhere very beautiful.

GREG. This doesn't sound like you. Stacy.

STACY. It is me though. I am going to kill you, Gregory.

GREG. What?

MATT. But you can't be -

STACY. Oh, yes I can be. I shall collect all that money from your Mr. B.

MATT. But no, you see it -

STACY. It's been nice working for you, Mr. Larson. Sorry not to give you two weeks notice. (*Shoots him and he falls to the floor. MATT is stunned.*)

GREG. (*As she shoots.*) No, Stacy, you -

MATT. Stacy, you shot him!

STACY. I wasn't sure I'd have the courage.

MATT. But why? Why? You're all wrong. It's all wrong. There's no hit man. It's all a mistake, a con job.

GREG. (*Laughs and rises triumphantly.*) I win! I win! I win the bet.

MATT. What the hell?

GREG. I am the winner. I am so damned clever.

STACY. (*Laughs.*) He fell for it. I can't believe it. (*Puts gun down.*)

MATT. But you mean you two planned this?

GREG. Of course we did.

MATT. (*Goes below GREG to STACY.*) You're a Benedict Arnold. A Judas Iscariot, a - a -

STACY. Mata Hari?

MATT. Yes, that too.

STACY. I am first and foremost a loyal employee and when you had me get that check for fifty thousand dollars I had to tell Greg.

GREG. (*Sits in chair C.*) And we took it from there. We decided we'd con you like you were trying to con me.

MATT. (*Between them.*) But you acted so well. All the time you -

STACY. (*Sits on the bench.*) That's because you had this place wired, didn't you?

GREG. We had to keep up the act even when we were alone.

MATT. I do have this evening on tape and I was going to play it at parties for years.

STACY. Poor boy.

I BET YOUR LIFE

GREG. And now you had better pay off all those people you hired out there, your cast of characters.

STACY. I must say they did very well.

MATT. They should. They're all actors. I found most of them on the unemployment line. (*Goes to windows.*)

GREG. It was rather obvious they were not real when not one of them reacted to the gunshot.

MATT. I told them to be prepared for anything, but I didn't expect a real shot. (*Calls outside.*) You can come in now. Curtain. The show is over. (*Comes back into the room.*)

GREG. (*Rises happily.*) I won! I won! I won!

MATT. You did not. You didn't figure out who the hit man was.

GREG. I did. It was Stacy.

MATT. But you put her up to it.

STACY. That doesn't matter. I was a hit person.

GREG. So there was no seedy bar, no Mr. B., no limousine accident and I still found a hit man. I won the bet.

MATT. I'm calling my lawyer. Arbitration. We'll go to arbitration.

HENRIETTA. (*Enters followed by IRA and goes above sofa.*) Do we get a curtain call?

IRA. (*Beside her.*) Or applause?

HENRIETTA. I'm not used to so much ad libbing when I do commercials. I like a script.

BURTON. (*Enters.*) Maybe I can get one of those stopped sink commercials where they use a plumber. I have the outfit.

GREG. You fooled me.

LILA. (*Enters. She drops her arch quality, goes below BURTON to C.*) I'm glad that's over. I don't think my character was very nice.

MATT. You did beautifully.

LILA. Maybe we could -

MATT. Yes. I'll speak to the casting agent and I'll write you a small part. If you do well the role could grow.

LILA. All I need is a chance.

LAURA. (*Comes in from D.L.*) How about me? These down home folks are my specialty.

HENRIETTA. Mine too, but you do the real natives better than I.

LAURA. Thanks.

MATT. I do want to thank you all for this most unusual job. Stacy here will have your check in the mail first thing tomorrow. I believe you have your car here, don't you, Ira?

IRA. Yes. I'll drive you all back to the city.

GREG. But Lila's car?

LILA. It was part of the gag.

GREG. Of course, I do applaud you all.

HENRIETTA. But what about the other one out there moaning under the tree?

GREG. We forgot about her.

IRA. I've never worked with her before.

LAURA. She's very good.

BURTON. A natural like Julie Harris.

GREG. Where is she?

GERTA. (*Enters still carrying the script.*) She is here. She is feeling negative. She is disillusioned.

MATT. She is not one of us.

GERTA. I am one of none.

GREG. You didn't hire her?

MATT. Not that I remember. *(To her.)* You were so good you will get a check anyway.

GERTA. Money, what is that?

HENRIETTA. I could tell you, dear.

GERTA. I am not discouraged. I shall come into your office, Mr. Larson., with my book. I shall not be there for several weeks as I shall have to walk back to the city. I do not believe in mass transit. I wish I could say it has been a pleasure meeting you all but it hasn't. Perhaps another time, another life. *(Exits with a moan.)*

LILA. I'd hate to share a dressing room with that one.

LAURA. I've worked with ingenues like that.

IRA. *(Goes U.C.)* Come along all, the car awaits.

LILA. *(To MATT.)* I do hope I'll be hearing from you.

MATT. You all will receive a casting call before much longer.

BURTON. If you don't call us we'll call you . *(They all laugh.)*

IRA. I suggest we all stop at this little bar I know on West 12th Street and have a cast party.

HENRIETTA. Come to my place. I have a condo at Lincoln Center. *(All ad-lib agreement.)*

IRA. *(At U.C.)* Can you join us?

GREG. No, thanks, we have the house for the weekend.

IRA. Here we go. My Honda chariot awaits. *(They all exit.)*

MATT. *(As they go.)* The cast departs.

STACY. Do you suppose Gerta with hitch-hike and they'll pick her up?

GREG. No, that one will walk and she'll be in the Guinness Book of Records and get on talk shows and make a fortune.

MATT. (*Sits on sofa still amazed.*) I cannot believe I was taken in by you two and I had it all so perfectly arranged. I even had Stacy and Laura rehearsed about the car wreck.

STACY. And I had stage fright when I made the call to the hospital.

MATT. You are not only a mole in my organization but it is time you came in out of the cold.

MATT. (*Goes to him.*) If she hadn't come to me do you think I would have fallen for your story about a hit man?

MATT. You would have but I wouldn't.

GREG. You fell for Stacy being a hit person, didn't you?

MATT. Only for a moment. It was the shock.

STACY. But you don't think I could be that type of girl, do you?

MATT. Never.

GREG. Not you.

STACY. How right you are. I could not kill you -

GREG. Of course not.

STACY. - unless forced to do so. (*Circles to L. of desk.*) But I could take advantage of you.

GREG. I've been hoping you would for ages.

STACY. I did get you to sign that check to fool Matt, didn't I?

GREG. Yes.

STACY. And it is long enough ago to have been cashed. Isn't it?

GREG. Yes.

STACY. And that could be squirreled away in a numbered account by now, couldn't it?

GREG. But it isn't, is it?

MATT. I think she is serious.

I BET YOUR LIFE

STACY. I know I am serious. (*Picks up the gun from the desk an we now see a much tougher STACY.*) The first was a blank, the second isn't but then I would hate to use this.

GREG. (*Both men rise.*) You're kidding?

STACY. (*Deadly serious.*) No, I am not.

MATT. She is not.

STACY. (*Backs U.C.*) What a grand life I shall have with all that money. Of course you both could try to stop me but think of the bad publicity for you. No, you're both too conceited to stop me.

GREG. Are we?

MATT. Yes, we are.

STACY. You think I have such a wonderful time working for you all day and being fought over by both of you the rest of the time. Did it ever occur to you I want more out of life? I wish I could say this hurts me more than it does you, but it doesn't.

GREG. You'll have our money and a bad conscience but you'll be all alone.

MATT. And lonely.

STACY. Not quite. You don't see me every night of the week. I'd like you to meet my fiancé. (*Calls off.*) You can come back in now.

BURTON. (*Strolls U.C.*) Hi, fellas.

MATT. Burton.

GREG. How did this happen?

STACY. It's been happening for a long time.

BURTON. (*His arm around her.*) You both think you're so smart but it's this little lady here that has the brains. Come on, let's get out of here.

STACY. What was it Gerta said - perhaps another time, another life? So long suckers. *(They exit and GREG and MATT sit on sofa.)*

GREG. Who would of thought?

MATT. Stacy, dear sweet Stacy.

GREG. What do they say in all those French farces, we've been cuckold?

MATT. The proper term is cuckolded. Anyway, I won the bet.

GREG. You did not.

MATT. You didn't guess the hit man.

GREG. It was Stacy.

MATT. But you put her up to it the first time.

GREG. And I didn't realize she would really be one. All right, I'll peddle your script. It does have a ring of truth.

MATT. I guess we deserve to be left alone, don't we?

GREG. I guess so.

MATT. We're just another odd couple.

STACY. *(As they both sigh, she comes bounding in the windows.)* Look at you two damn stupid fools.

GREG. Stacy!

MATT. Back again?

STACY. You fell for it, didn't you?

GREG. You mean -

MATT. You're not - you didn't.

STACY. *(Goes above sofa.)* You have been so busy conning each other you didn't realize I was conning both of you. Oh, what a triumph for womankind.

GREG. But Burton -

STACY. *(Goes C.)* I met with him last week when he came by the office and arranged the whole thing. He said it was a good chance to audition for you.

GREG. My brain is swimming.

STACY. So here we are, the three of us with our consciences all clear.

MATT. But Greg did say he would peddle the script to the coast.

GREG. With a few rewrites.

MATT. Such as?

GREG. A twist. A better twist.

STACY. How about -?

MATT. Suppose the leading lady turns out to be conning both men?

GREG. It's not plausible.

STACY. Oh, no.

MATT. *(Rises and goes to STACY C.)* Of course it is. It just happened.

GREG. *(Rises.)* That's right. We could have the ingenue actually be carrying on with this third man and -

STACY. I should have had this copyrighted.

GREG. - and you could make her more a fallen woman.

MATT. That gives us a chance for some sex and violence, got to have sex and violence.

STACY. *(During above, goes to the dining room doorway.)* I'll put on the coffee. It's going to be a long night. *(She exits as*

CURTAIN

PROPERTY LIST

ACT I

Preset: phone, pad, pencil on desk, phone book in desk drawer

Down Right:
2 grocery bags of food (LAURA)
Overly large, battered script (GERTA)
Purse with card (HENRIETTA)

Up Right:
Attaché case, purse (STACY)
2 suitcases (GREG)
Metal tool chest with wrench (BURTON)
Work order (BURTON)
Plumber's manual (BURTON)

Off Left:
Highball (STACY)
Tablecloth folded (LAURA)
2 highballs (GREG)
Set of napkins (LAURA)
Bud vase with one flower (LAURA)
Tray with silverware and plates (LAURA)

ACT II

Preset: remove glasses, check pistol in STACY'S purse on desk

Down Right:
Napkin (IRA)

Off left:
Plate of egg rolls (Can be covered) (LAURA)
Glass of water (LILA)
Covered salad bowl (LAURA)
Covered bread tray (LAURA)
Covered butter dish (LAURA)

www.ingramcontent.com/pod-product-compliance
Lightning Source LLC
Chambersburg PA
CBHW072019290426
44109CB00018B/2282